Uses of My Body

Simone Savannah

Cover Art: *Summer 1988* by Maylleline Espinosa
Art Direction by Laura Marciano
Designed by Michelle Caraccia

Published 2020 by Barrow Street, Inc.
(501) (c) 3) corporation. All contributions are tax deductible.
Distributed by:
    Barrow Street Books
    P.O. Box 1558
    Kingston, RI 02881

Barrow Street Books are also distributed by Small Press Distribution, SPD, 1341
Seventh Street Berkeley, CA 94710-1409, spd@spdbooks.org; (510) 524-1668,
(800) 869-7553 (Toll-free within the US); amazon.com; Ingram Periodicals Inc.,
1240 Heil Quaker Blvd, PO Box 7000, La Vergne, TN 37086-700 (615) 213-
3574; and Armadillo & Co., 7310 S. La Cienega Blvd, Inglewood, CA 90302,
(310) 693-6061.

Special thanks to the University of Rhode Island English Department and
especially the PhD Program in English, 60 Upper College Road, Swan 114,
Kingston, RI 02881, (401) 874-5931, which provides valuable in-kind support,
including graduate and undergraduate interns.

First Edition

Library of Congress Control Number: 2020943309

ISBN 978-0-9997461-8-9

Uses of My Body

Simone Savannah

Barrow Street Press
New York City

for my mother and sisters

CONTENTS

Acknowledgments

Poem related to my body

Though I am a poet, I am often mistaken for a sprinter.

Today, a man at the gas station watched me
walk behind his car and asked, "you go to school here?"
"you look like you ran track like a mu'fucka!"

It is mostly my quads I think: these twin
four-headed muscles,
22 inches around
prefer isolation
deep squats
have pressed and quivered
resisted heavy weight,
the academy,
white women I teach in Pilates
who ask if they can touch them.

A black woman I met at the bar
joked about the girth of my arms.
She asked why I work out so much
if I am just a writer and teacher
not the hurdler she thinks I am.

I want to write the book about my body
something that speaks
to the way I am actually built
have moved and pushed
have drenched myself in sweat.

Sleeping

Once you texted me from Arizona
a picture of a comforter with the words
her side written on a large black space that
takes up most of the big bed and
his side written on the white space remaining.
You wrote, "Lol this made me think of you"

When you were in Kansas, you pretended
to be falling off the bed
because I had my whole body spread
across the mattress.
You never told me
you loved me for it, but you made me laugh
and laugh about it.
I think when you texted me
you really wanted to say
"Lol I still need you"
the way I take up space
a cold piece of work, and
though I never let you hold me
you used to call me
woman.

Preclude

There is sex on my Instagram.
I like to be sex on my Instagram.
Like to look like a witch and say cute shit
about the man I've been sleeping with—
        I tell him I like him when I like his shit.

We text about sex sometimes. Have sex there sometimes.

Screen protector like a condom
or coconut oil on the clitoris.
I say shit like baby,
let me slurp down that big ass dick.
But, sometimes I just spit on the tip
on some cute ass shit.

I send nudes with my locs and my eyes cut out—
Please, white boys, don't break my iCloud;
Job market got restrictions on pussies that don't hide out—

Toward the body

I can't stop looking at children.
I keep picking them up and imagining they are mine:
their noses, their fingers, the way the little girl's eyes
have taken the shape of chocolate almonds.
If her name is Aniyah or Olivia, I know God is fucking with me.
I pick her up. I wanted to kiss her, but just tickle her arms
so her mother doesn't think I am lonely or begging—

I still have the panties I wore five years ago.
They are pink and stained.
The nurse was brown and pregnant and offered me a cookie.
I laughed but I cannot remember if I took it.
I know it was chocolate and had cream in the middle.
I know she made me sign one last piece of paper
and told me where to find the exit.

Sometimes in public I caress the whole of my belly
I imagine I am lying across the bed in B's duplex
as he searches for abortion clinics and writes down prices.
I imagine that my breasts are leaking white onto his bed,
or that six and a half weeks is too late to do anything about it.

B wanted confirmation.
He wouldn't take off work to witness
the detachment
the cloth colored jar I wanted to see into—

These days when he asks me how I feel
I tell him he still owes me money for the procedure.

Like want for having

Sometimes it is the yellow, spotted bananas
on my refrigerator that make me think of you—
not for your touch or for the chocolate, but because
of the time you went to work and left me at your place,
said that if I got hungry,
that I could have anything I wanted.

I thought if you had bananas, I would crump dance in
    your kitchen.
but, no, you did not have bananas, so I ate your peanuts and
    drank your
last bottle of water, thought about how you said
I could have anything.

        I wondered if hunger is   why women get married,
        not for the bananas,
        but for the company and for the having of absolutely
            anything.

I wonder now, if hunger is   why men send me
    strange messages
about how they want to spit in my throat,
or call me baby or sweetheart and ask me

to say what I want
to do with their dicks and my tongue—

I have only wanted to eat *you*
and ripe bananas, and sometimes only want
you and I dancing in your living room,
taking shots of red bull and 1800
like you have no idea
I conjured you.

If my mother were alive

If my mother were alive, we'd talk about our men.
We'd laugh, throw our heads back and push
each other at the shoulders, say remember the man
you left early in the morning the day you got dad
to say that he was gay so that whatshisname wouldn't
think you were still sleeping with him.
She'd tell me that not all men can be conquered that easily.
She had wanted to really be loved by a man
but they only sought her because she was beautiful.

My second cousin calls me Tracy sometimes.
She says I sound like my mother when I laugh.
And she says I don't take men seriously either:
I only want to fuck them.
I want to tell her it's because I am black and a woman.
I want a chance at my own body.
Mommy's surgery was her having a chance at her own body
She fucked men because we all have learned to fuck men.
But I think Pam knows all of this.
She is a black woman too.
She knows the lives of men because each of the men she married
died—widowed her.

She tries not to remember running
to the alley and discovering bullet holes
in her second husband's chest.

I want to know why my mother wanted the surgery
positioned herself as fixable.

body dancer

for years I was a dancer

learning to use my body from a tall brown woman named Ms. April.

She is the first woman who taught me

to isolate my hips

to lift my sternum

to balance the chakras with breath

to balance the body

       in flat backs and jazz turns—

What a coincidence, a few weeks ago I found her on Facebook

living near Kansas City. I want to know if she remembers me

when I began and when I quit all of a sudden in the middle of
    her Summer Intensive—

I want to ask her if she could teach me again

to be whole

give me permission to leap

to exist between vinyl and page and sound and body and grit

to sweat my yearning—

My mother is dead.

The one who sewed her two African-print pillows is dead or
    died too soon.

She stopped sewing with her hands and her breath—

I don't ever want anything

or even my own body to stop me

the way my mother was stopped.

queen

Today, on my walk to the gas station for a Swisher and a bottle of water, a group of men call at me from across the street. I look at them and shake my head, and when I come out of the store, I know one of them will drive their big blue truck across the street to find and follow me, and yes they pull up on me: the man with the gold horse teeth stops cuts me off with the big blue truck and they say *it's okay, it's okay, we not gon hurt you,* and their words echo, and a man in a neon green short sleeve shirt and matching shoes and a blue hat and square sunglasses and big round eyes gets out of the big blue truck and tells the driver with the horse teeth he can park, and he asks me my name and I tell him my name, my real name because I don't want to appear afraid, and he says something about him working up at the school and he asks me if he can see me sometimes, and I want to tell this nigga to get the fuck up out my face but I tell him I have a man so he gets the message, but he still asks for my number and I tell him I'll take his instead and he asks the other man with the short hair waves and sweaty wrinkled brow to throw him his phone (he does not move his body, he keeps peering over his sunglasses with his big round eyes at me) and then he tells me something that begins with 601 and I save it as Del because he says that's his name, and he asks me for a hug and I tell him *no,* and he

says *that's okay I'll take one, I'll take uh hug,* and I cringe when
he stoops down and wraps his arms and bitter cologne around
my body, and I see the two men in the truck watching and I
want to know what they wonder about men and power, about
why their man wanted to touch me so badly—

after he uncloaks his body from my breasts and shoulders,
he walks away and says *sawry bu' we saw uh beautiful black
queen and I jus had tuh say hi, you'uh beautiful black woman,*
and the men in the truck smile with their chins hanging and
ask me if I have any *cuhzins.*

Personal, or how do I write about this shit in a dissertation

In 2009, Ohio, I got pregnant the day or a few days after my nephew was born. A few months later my godfather asked if I had a poem for a liberation event on campus—I told him I had a poem for the way B made me cum real hard then begged me to have my first child vacuumed out of me and only gave me a hundred dollars when I needed four hundred—I have a ritual for disregarding men's pockets and feelings now. For example a year later, B told me we shouldn't have done it. And I said naw, that was all me, my nigga—not you—parts of my body: emptied and jarred.

After the gym

Tonight I ran 2 miles at the gym then went to see
the weed man. He is a tall white lanky thing
who always packs a fourth into a Ziploc bag for me.
I think he is sexy because he moves
slowly and looks me in the eye when he takes my cash.
I always smile at him and imagine us fucking—
I think I must like white men, too.
Tonight I am sitting in the middle of my bed
surrounded by crystals. I believe I am a witch:
living off moons and vibrations.
Smoking the purple he gave me
running back Alice Walker lines, I think maybe it will
piss God off if I don't
notice myself, too: the way my thighs *have come*
to look like an athlete's thighs—
I remember the time a white woman looked me up and down
while I was getting dressed in the gym's locker room.
She said I must have always been this thin and pretty.
She joked how she'd keep her man from me if he were still alive.
Tonight I remember that I used to dream of only dancing and
the way a leotard might fit me now, or even jazz shoes.
I've wanted to be a famous woman—
books written about the use of my body.

Not without Kansas

It is when I am in Kansas
that laughter enters me through the shoulders
makes me stain your chocolate couch
with coconut-oil arches...

There we do herb rituals—mimic earth to fire...

my small coughs mimic your love energy stuttering back
to you.

You feel like my only God
when your tongue swipes my touch
when you make me mimic my own vibrations
or stir me.

There we have children that laugh like us
I make love to you with my hands at the edge of
my mouth.

I want to say something about loving you
but gargle your kiss in my throat—

Years after you die

My father told me that a man kicked you
in the stomach once. It was hard enough
to put you in the hospital
where he told you he wanted to put a bullet through
the man's head once he found him.

He said *he* even tried to break down your door
banged at it for you so hard
the neighbors called the police.
He had to hide
somewhere in an alley in the dark
all because he thought some other man
was up there with you.
He was always with you
even when you were with someone else—
my stepfather for instance
whom he is angry with
for having babies with you
while he was away in prison.

You were once a security guard
but at home men broke you again and again
the man you sold dope for broke you
my grandfather broke you
my sisters' fathers broke you
my brothers' fathers broke you
the doctor broke you open.
There is something you wanted
taken out of you I think
something as quick as the breath—
you gave birth so many times
it was easy for you to die.

In April I visited your mother's grave.
I know you went looking for her in Cleveland the year after
    I was born.
Your mother's grave is mostly brown grass.
There is no headstone to identify her or to say how long she
    lived or had been dying.
The attendants put out a purple flag with her name and plot
    number
that I took home and placed next to a photo of you.
Do you wonder what she thinks of you now: dead, too,
your daughter looking for you, for some garden of yours?
Do you think she'd say something about the way
men tell stories now that her body
has settled in hard ground?
Or about much she ached and ached—
I don't know if she actually ached
I know something must have driven her crazy
the way they say she went crazy.

You and I could be sisters
how long we've been without our mothers.

I have resisted

I have resisted
naming my dissertation after the sex and the personal:
I fuck my men so good: poems
I want to apologize to my neighbors
but black women have never been able to fuck
so loudly or shout about it when it isn't demanded from the body—
I only fuck if the dick is political.
Today the dick is good and heavy
asks me questions like
will I keep fucking him until he comes?

Like the time for wanting, Ohio

Sometimes I am lying across my couch in Kansas
texting you: *I want to do the things we used to do*
like the time I came home and met you in a hotel
after your sister's wedding
where you said you missed me, that I never stay
in Ohio long enough, and asked why
I stopped eating at Waffle House with you.

Mostly I said I wanted a different body.
Mostly you said you'll always want me.
Even when you're married, you'll still fuck with me—
like the time you spent a week with me in Kansas
watching *Star Trek* and episodes of *Cosmos*
my body mostly in the smoke in your hands,
though you have a woman in Ohio you've told all ten years
we've been just friends, or too close for her to know the
    difference—

I like never having to birth your children
or really put up with you,
though I do want to ask
why you want me so much
but not at all—

I am not a good woman
I still want you to do
what you used to do to me.

limber

Look
splits so deep
my pussy lips kiss
the blue yoga mat / I came up in here with
bitch   you so average:
cat cows / backbends / sun salutations: gained

I : born this way : double-dutched double-jointed blood /
   black girl / Gabby girl / black magic
thick thighs yes stretch too   hips mimic elastic /I : breathe
   and slip / sustain
the weight of your instructions in my wrists—
in child's pose I   worship Misty's
tip   toe   ball pointed calves
ask her to   forgive me   for
          being
                    here
and no longer
          dancing

before
you want me : eyes locked on my contortion
say *how beautifully limber*
then, you: yoga trained / body forced / skin thinned
flip through Yoga Journal / study my *hypermobility*:
practice my body in your bedroom mirror /tell me
*watch your knees / try not to hyperextend /*rise
to correct me / say I must
get headaches from good sex and stretching /say
also *be sure to level your hips* / as if
it is my first time / blooming into half moons
you couldn't imagine

you think
God must have birthed broken brown bodies
forgot to thread the joints of all the blue black trap niggas—

Look here : I'm a don't-need-a-strap-nigga
core strength so live
padangusthasana so steady /twisted
in eagle pose/ my eyes closed/ you watch me
         I used to exhale into a standing split/ when I used to
            strip/ tipped
twenties stuck to the back of my thighs/ still
not afraid of my body:
yoga right next to you
like I'm your 500-hour teacher
last name like your Savasana
yoga right next to you
cuz
I'm even savage in mudras

and yo ya man in the back
always twists his neck to see me without permission—
after class told me he can't help but watch me in the mirror
wanted to know what else stretches that wide—
sweetheart how long you been into this
'cause you do it so   easy
wondered if I saw Serena's match that day
you must be her sister Venus, he said
body
a hot
yoga train of flesh
he reached out to touch me

Morning

When I awoke this morning
I immediately wanted the red wine I began
before going to sleep last night.
I skipped meditation and just journaled.
I asked God why I didn't settle last night:
take the white man home to fuck him.
I rewatched an episode of *Broad City*, the one where
Abby and Alana confront patriarchy and Western medicine
then I remembered I left my coconut curry
behind at the restaurant.
I wonder if he will be there tonight with some other woman
talking universe, how he reads seven books at once
(15 minutes a day on each book).
I wonder if he would bore the fuck out of her.

By afternoon one of the men I used to love in Ohio
asked me about the dinner after I posted my food on Facebook.
He said nothing about me has changed:
that I still go on dates just to get fucked.
I have not responded to his messages.
I have no feminist response, no black feminist response.
He is just trying to be important.
He wants his sleepy eyes on my breasts and
his baby momma with my name in her mouth.

When I prayed this morning,
I told God I want my last lover
because he said he knew me for real.
He always had a smile and brown skin for me at his door.
He always fucked me and said thank you.
The first time we met, we stood at each other's bodies
talking directions and humidity.
He said he wanted me
because he saw me standing
with my hip out in the middle of Kansas.

Personal, or how do I write about this shit in a dissertation

The second time I watched Spike Lee's *She's Gotta Have It*, I was in an undergraduate feminist film course where we read bell hooks who argued Nola Darling isn't free at all—her unabashed sexuality was written by men for men trying to clear their names.

My white classmates said, "poor black girl" or something similar and my professor said, "yes / race / woman / looked-at-ness" and we began marking the moments at which Nola's body is not on screen or being touched. Nola's body is everywhere / always being touched.

I am not sure if I am Nola Darling or not Nola Darling, or trying to resist being Nola Darling, over-determined / written to be gazed at / trying to gaze back but raped for it. My body is mine, but many men, too, will say they've had it because they have had it, or they want me to promise them my body. Academia makes me write a dissertation to clear my name:

I begin: I am not a jezebel. My body has been made up. My erotic has been made up.

And actually: I am or want to be angry about it, some attempt at a blues woman. I read poems to remake the self. I write poems to remake the self.

My mother tried to remake her body, but died as soon as she began.

When my mother was decay

On the morning of her surgery, my mother picked me up
from my cousin's house and gave me Oreos, a parting gift,
as if she knew she was going to die, but she didn't die
immediately. That day my family and I saw her new body:
still large and brown and her eyes still big
sleepy and numb from the anesthesia.
We had expected the surgery to work right away.

We did not expect her to stay in the hospital for seven months,
for her ankles to swell, the medical socks, the smell of decay and
open blisters and gauzes when her left breast turned rock solid
            and black.
We did not anticipate the amputation, her long breasts as
            removable,
the use of skin from her thigh to cover the phantom
            complication of fleshy white.
My mother told us she wanted her flesh (gone), her stomach
            (the size of an egg),
her thighs (gaping) and her body (so slim and tender it would
            slide from the bone).
When, instead, her body began to
            loosen,
when her skin began dragging slow and dry and cracking at
            the incisions,
she still laughed, squealed and opened her mouth so wide the
            wind
knocked her head back. And yes, the men still came.
They weren't particular about bodies or death or hospital beds—
On the day she died, they all showed up demanding to be her
            husband on paper.
T reasoned that he was the last to fuck her, but
we chose my stepfather because he was the last to give her
            children.

My mother: said she would die when she was thirty-six,
but she was actually thirty-seven, so we delayed the wake and
          built a casket
that would fit her still large body.
We dressed her in white and sewed her eyes shut
so the medicine wouldn't leak and disturb the congregation.
The mortician also said we needed to buy a sock to stuff her
          bra and
gloves to hide her blistered hands.

We buried my mother's body eight days into September
in the soil of a cemetery on 17th avenue, and ate soul food in
          the basement
of the church and some at my grandfather's house where he
          showed me a picture
of my birth grandmother (dead at 37), and he said she was
          crazy
had drank herself into a closet to break and die alone.
He said he was sorry he had given Tracy up.
          His limp and his heart were too heavy to help carry
          her casket,
but he remembered holding my mother the day she was
          born.

On the day of her death, the actual day, I watched my mother
          die for a while.
I held her hands beneath the blankets in ICU while my
          aunts sung to her.
They told her she could let go and go home if she wanted.
When the doctor said she had less than an hour, I looked
          at the clock
above her head, then back at the blood seeping out of her nose
          and ears.

My eldest brother and I left her body with my aunts at the
          hospital:
still large, now shuddering like she had just begun to fear the
          decay.

On the day of my mother's death, the actual day, we faced the
          hot August
Sunday from the porch where my brother said it was all fucked
          up
grilled chicken breasts and carved the round
          shape of her face
into my grandparents' wooden stairs.
He left the porch for a Swisher and soda
and returned with cookies. I thought
          she wouldn't die at all.
But after my aunt called, and after my
          stepfather came
home with her things: her gown, and the OSU hospital cup
          with her lipstick
on tip of the straw, it became true.

Like Kansas

This morning I am in Kansas
finishing the last of the blunt
we shared.
"I'm high" you said
and we stopped smoking to make love with our tongues and
 our breaths—

But, this is not Kansas
just its Topeka and humidity—
can't
call out your name now | say *baby* to you |
ease myself onto your dick again |feel inside
me again magic| or my body responding
to your body | squirt spells on your belly

I don't want to fuck anyone else until I fuck you again:
have your spit dripping toward my nipples | your dick
tapping my teeth| your magic in my throat |
your magic on my cheek
again

I want to be on top of you or near you until my body
convulses or pretends it can't speak—

I want to chain smoke fire with you so I can lick the ashes
from your fingertips | have you lick the nectar from my
 fingertips |
have you swallow the laughter from my fingertips
until we are high enough to really
pray to God—

to ask Her to make time the same time
and make distance a place in the middle
like Kansas

My thing with B

When I arrived at my ex-baby father's brother's house
he had on a big smile and he hugged me
until it was clear he wanted me.
He said *look how long and pretty your hair has gotten since I last*
   seen you in '09.
When I looked up at him
smiled at his dark brown
to tell him THANK YOU,
he said *girl   you turn me on.*
I asked him *even after my thing with B?* because I wanted him to know
how nasty he is.
He said *even before that*
like it was about timing—

he expected he could wet me up
would get to come in me
thought he could make my honey sweeter
dip and twist his late dick in abortion blood   or abortion cum
that he, too, would spill his liquid white
because he couldn't somehow do it before B
or before the thing.

Kris and I in Graduate School

Kris and I talk over loose-leaf green tea and rose at her house.

We talk yoni steams: draping skirts and our bodies over boiling pots

of rosemary calendula lavender and yarrow in the middle of

　　graduate school.

We talk toning the uterus, reproduction, birthing babies, the

　　raspberry leaf

for her cramping, and we talk 26-day cycles of blood and

　　contractions and how

to balance the ovaries. We talk damiana and cervical mucus,

　　the coming,

and Kris, she apologizes for having left her panties on her

　　bathroom floor.

Kris and I take a break from our brown skin,

or we return to it and take a trip to the natural grocer

and we grab more than the almond milk and black beans

　　for dinner—

we talk aloe vera for healing and throw it in the cart we share

and we think to buy the dandelion detox tea because sometimes

the warm lemon water in the morning isn't enough to release

the poison we still sometimes consume.

Kris and I see royal jelly and talk about how much in a daily dosage

and we talk fertility and having babies again.

And Kris says I should have a baby and I think she should

    have a baby:

fill ours wombs with honey and semen and limbs and other parts

    of our children

so we grab the royal jelly from its shelf and find winter oils

to protect our growing skin & hair.

Body in the Locker Room

In the locker room we are all naked or wrapped in white towels
towels too small to fit my thick ass frame
so I have to tie the white towel mostly at the waist and let
   my brown
titties bounce out loud in front of white women and mirrors.

In the mirror I am the only black body. The two Latina women
   tease each other
tease each other's brown bodies, say to each other, *you white as*
   fuck today,
replace brown for pale and talk about tanning as I laugh and
   polish my tender
brown skin with coconut oil and take down my hair.

The white woman next to me asks how long I've been growing it
says she has always wondered
how [black women] do that shit—tie their coarse black hair
 . in knots.
She asks if she can touch it.
I tell the bitch *no* and want to ask her if she learned that shit
   in White women's studies—
I want to ask the bitch if she went to college, if she took her
   white body to college

if she knew black women don't play that shit—
She asks why I'm so angry
like all she wanted to do was touch.

Yearn Time

When I watched *Waiting to Exhale*
with my girl cousins Tasha and Kourtney
they said I had to play Robin
so I anticipated the married men
the abortion, the blood, references to the *lady in blue*—
Everyone who knew I was pregnant
told me to keep it.
I did not keep it
though it hurt to be there in the room alone
to have him waiting for me to say I'd done it—

Just days after the procedure
I wanted to be pregnant again

but now sometimes I say
I took care of that shit
that I will never give birth
to a stupid nigga's baby.

Re-Memory 28

After twenty-eight years my sister has come up
Her body is large and brown like my mother's.
Her locs are palm-rolled like mine—
she cut them off when they became shoulder-length.
We discussed the dream she had about how heavy they made
her.

Tiffany (now Tiffani) and I were both given the middle name
    Nicole
after our mother's best friend Nicki.
We were almost womb partners, almost twins
just ten months apart.
There are twenty-eight years before I look her in the eye
for the first time.
She tells me my mother almost gave me up, too.

When we finally talked about it, my eldest brother said
my mother giving up our sister
said everything about why I was born and kept.
I think I must haunt my sister
since our mother is dead.

does one heal from domestic violence

did your mother succumb to the abuse : a blunt object
specifically : a thick glass bottle to the head on an early Tuesday
morning after an argument when she finally had enough / broke
it off / said the relationship no longer served her / an affirmation
she had practiced—

or was that you at the death of an exhausting love :
each heavy clash
your lover blows against your skull
you scream
smell your mother
being buried

Body Craft

The white woman who teaches
my weight lifting class approached me
in the locker room while I was at the sink
applying rose hip oil to my cheeks.
She asked if I am still tutoring football players
They couldn't possibly take you seriously—
you're so pretty, she said.

The former football player who fucks
me sometimes says I am a witch because
I make my own cuticle strengthener:
equal amounts of almond, rice bran,
jojoba, and five drops of lavender
essential oil in a small mason jar.
When he took down my panties
in the middle of my living room
he said I think I must be the shit
because I was dressed in all
black and had my long nails painted
black in the middle of winter.

Kansas, continued in winter

there is no dick for black women

in Kansas.

too many of my bitches here text me:

bitch, the dick not thick enough or

the dick good

but not good enough or

sis, where is the sex for a bitch

who's a healer?

once a nigga here

said my pussy felt like home.

ask me

if he ever made me come.

Where to begin for the answers

When I learned Tiffani and I
are only ten months apart I had questions
for my father that I can't ask my mother
because she is dead.

I discovered one of Tiffany's adoption search forms on the
    Internet.
She began looking for answers at 15
searching only with the description the court gives her at birth:
our mother is black and female
her father is tall.

wanting

I am late to work today.
I have wanted to spend the morning
taking my time at the gym
taking my time to make love to myself.
Each rep of a deadlift makes me feel so strong—
At work I pretend I can carry all tasks given to me
without thinking about myself.
The day I ordered a small power wand
between meetings with students
I felt like I could do anything I wanted
though I do ask myself when will I
have babies or just one baby
or if it is really true that I want someone
other than myself.

Notes on pleasure

the nurse called the tissue / sticking out of my ring finger : a defensive wound / she was surprised by my survival / that I did not go / unconscious under your attack

At my last visit my therapist asked : what is it like to have once loved you / to have let you love me : I think he meant to ask what is it like / to have loved /the person who abused you/ battled your body

mostly I said it is like being manipulated / not even being able to grieve the sex / without fighting myself / your strange fist balled up / turning over and over inside me / I beg myself / not to become wet / or mostly sick / throw up at memories of being pleasured by you

I still want to burn up your shit / the clothes you left in my baskets / your vision board torn beneath my bed now / even the only picture of your dead grandmother in her youth / I still want to drop the plant / you gifted me / over the balcony outside of my third-floor apartment / I want the ceramic to shatter / the shiny petals to tear / on the thorns of concrete roses

however / I have named her / have repotted her in a bigger pot
since she began to tilt in the one you brought

Bloom Time

Mostly I lied to my therapist
when he asked if I had ever thought
about being unfaithful
to the woman I was with.
I mean how do I say
to this mindful ass white man:
I'm a bad woman
too, or I'm not so good
at being good to anybody.
In other words, I cheat on niggas
because they deserve it.
When I told my best friend I did it
because the relationship was heavy
a trauma I'd never imagined carrying and
I just wanted some hoe ass shit
popping in my apartment again,
he said *welcome back welcome back—you a bad bitch; beloved*
you can have anything you've wanted
I said you right you right.
I didn't leave her immediately
but I did leave.

Personal, or how do I write about this shit in a dissertation

I do not write poems about sex

because my orgasms are too short on the page

my nudes don't come out right

my man's dick is not hard enough in a poem

because my professor wants to fuck me

Sunday 9:19pm CT

when I take the blunt   touch your fingers   inhale
      send your laughter
      into my belly
I think about last Thursday:
pushing up to downward facing dog
watching the tips of my locs on the floor.
I let another man pick me up and
grip my thighs
just hours after you

today I wave the blunt back in your direction
touch your fingers
you tell me
I haven't smoked enough

Deliberate

Maybe she was deliberate.

Maybe she wanted to die

because her body weighed so heavy

on her brown or her man.

The surgery was never made to work for her.

being

beautiful: being black and a woman is difficult.

I must be deliberate, I know now.

Men (mis) read my dissertation /my poems / want to fuck me.

Men ask me if I am a witch / if I know magic

because my oils and my remedies sit on my bathroom

counter

and next to my bed / ready for use.

I could heal at any moment

make a body

soften / the uterus still with molasses and raspberry leaves.

A man in Texas said however it is mostly

my long hair and almond like eyes that made him

ask for me or demand I touch him

that my body is a prayer

the one where they won't ever do it again—

But these days I'm on my poetics

so heavy / my anger so deliberate

I'm like naw don't touch me and

fuck the woman who spread my nudes

across the internet then wanted me back.

She can't have me back.

Fuck the street that broke my mother

because I grew up there too:

the same men bother me / tell me I look just like her

and   Kansas / and every white bitch that has tried me

or has touched me.

and   the man who left me

in Kansas loving him:

I cried and I cried until he had a baby on me.

Now I'm like naw

'cause once you called me *woman*.

I know what commitment is.

Perhaps I'll die

unkept

or perhaps I enjoy being wanted

dead

maybe like my mother

whom I believe was so beautiful: at 8 I witnessed her staring

into her vanity mirror each morning

applying makeup and perfume

listening to Blackstreet / we sung together: don't leave me,

girl.

She left me.

A psychic: I believe she anticipated her death /

wrote it down for years in her journals

some erotic spell

my living: erotic

less about being wanted

alive now.

My mother refused to give me up the way

her mother gave her up

or the way she was made to give up Tiffany.

She doesn't kill me the way

I made blood

out of my first child who

I wanted—

Our wombs are not dangerous

wounded maybe.

Fact is B never deserved my children.

He still wants to come in me

even if it means I'd have to do it again.

Fisting

It is July for the sixth time in Kansas
when I begin wanting again—
I want peaches.
I want a job or a printer in my home.

I think I want to fuck men again—
No, I think I want to be fisted.

I asked my closest friend if she thinks
I am out of my mind for still imagining
being fucked by my ex who put their hands on me
while I play with myself

My friend said, *bitch please! If you came*
then shit, cum again

I mean it was everything—
sliding two, then three, then four fingers inside me before
    filling me up—
What should I do wanting my body to tick that way again?

How do you enter me so easy though it's been years?
How do I still cream white again and again on your hand
like I haven't had to fight you?

Notes on my bisexuality

some of the studs I've dated wanted to know
about my poems: who is the man that fucked me
that good, or if I am bisexual or if I am a lesbian.
The question is always would I leave for men
right in the middle of fucking them.

Ritual No. 30

today I showered and prayed over

my body for the first time in a long time

I told my godmother it is time, I want to be my own best

    thing—how do I begin?

She suggested lavender and honey tea

over turmeric and also asked if I've smudged my crystals lately—

No, I told her

then put a black obsidian yoni egg inside me and smoked weed

    all day.

I figure all I need is company sometimes

not to have my space invaded by love

that ain't love at all—how do I be angry

how do I come back to myself

or what I've always wanted?

How come there are so many women

in my private Facebook groups asking how to leave or move on?

When I asked my brother, he told me shit do it like mommy:

be blunt like the time she pulls out a 9 shot .22 on my stepfather

told him if Mrs. Bernadette's that good to him

then take his red ass down there and be with her, *you stupid*

    mothafucker.

I listen to podcasts each morning now
learn to laugh at men, then reread Ms. Sanchez
learn to gaze
at myself instead of turning away
learn to run myself water and bathe
and drink wine and make love to men
like a single woman

learn to become political about my yearning
erotic about my healing.

Acknowledgements

(some earlier versions of these poems appeared with different titles).

Apogee: "Black Girls"

Big Lucks: "Like Want for Having," "Morning"

Breakbeat Poets: Black Girl Magic: "Look"

GlitterMOB: "Prelude"

Ocean State Review: "Ritual No. 30," "When My Mother Was Decay"

Powder Keg Magazine: "Body in the Locker Room"

Puerto del Sol: "Kris and I in Graduate School," "Like Therapy for the men or the pleasure"

Shade Journal: "Not Without Kansas"

The Continental Review: "Years After You Die"

The Fem: "Toward The Body"

Vending Machine Press: "After the Gym," "Bloom Time," "Like Kansas," "Personal, or how do I write about this shit in a dissertation," "Sleeping"

Vinyl: "If My Mother Were Alive"

Voicemail Poems and Breakbeat Poets: Black Girl Magic: "queen"

Wus Good: "Does One Heal From Domestic Violence"

BARROW STREET POETRY

For the Fire from the Straw
Heidi Lynn Nilsson (2017)

Alma Almanac
Sarah Ann Winn (2017)

A Dangling House
Maeve Kinkead (2017)

Noon until Night
Richard Hoffman (2017)

Kingdom Come Radio Show
Joni Wallace (2016)

In Which I Play the Run Away
Rochelle Hurt (2016)

The Dear Remote Nearness of You
Danielle Legros Georges (2016)

Detainee
Miguel Murphy (2016)

Our Emotions Get Carried Away Beyond Us
Danielle Cadena Deulen (2015)

Radioland
Lesley Wheeler (2015)

Tributary
Kevin McLellan (2015)

Warranty in Zulu
Matthew Gavin Frank (2010)

Heterotopia
Lesley Wheeler (2010)

This Noisy Egg
Nicole Walker (2010)

Black Leapt In
Chris Forhan (2009)

Boy with Flowers
Ely Shipley (2008)

Gold Star Road
Richard Hoffman (2007)

Hidden Sequel
Stan Sanvel Rubin (2006)

Annus Mirabilis
Sally Ball (2005)

A Hat on the Bed
Christine Scanlon (2004)

Hiatus
Evelyn Reilly (2004)

3.14159+
Lois Hirshkowitz (2004)

Selah
Joshua Corey (2003)